I'm Going To READ!

OVER 200 FREQUENTLY USED WORDS

Sight Words

STERLING CHILDREN'S BOOKS
New York

In this book you will learn these kinds of words:

Colors

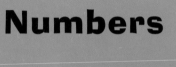

Numbers

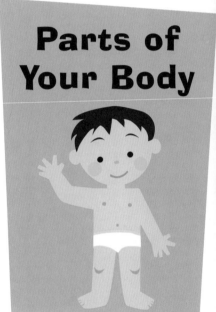

Parts of Your Body

Food

Months

Days

Weather

Shapes

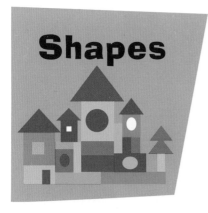

People

Signs

At the Office

At Home

Things That Go

Where?

Our World

Everyday Words

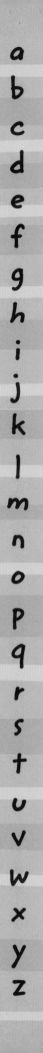

Colors

Trace and write.

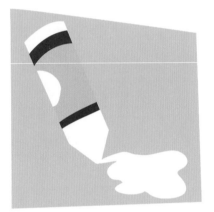

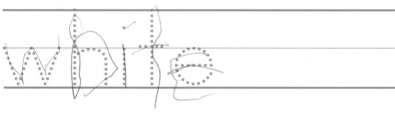
white

yellow

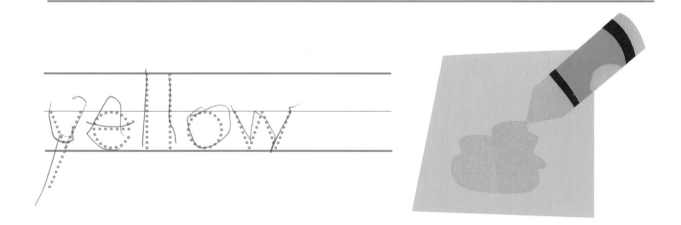

purple

brown

black

Numbers

Trace and write.

one

two

three

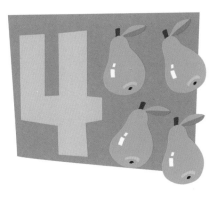

four

five

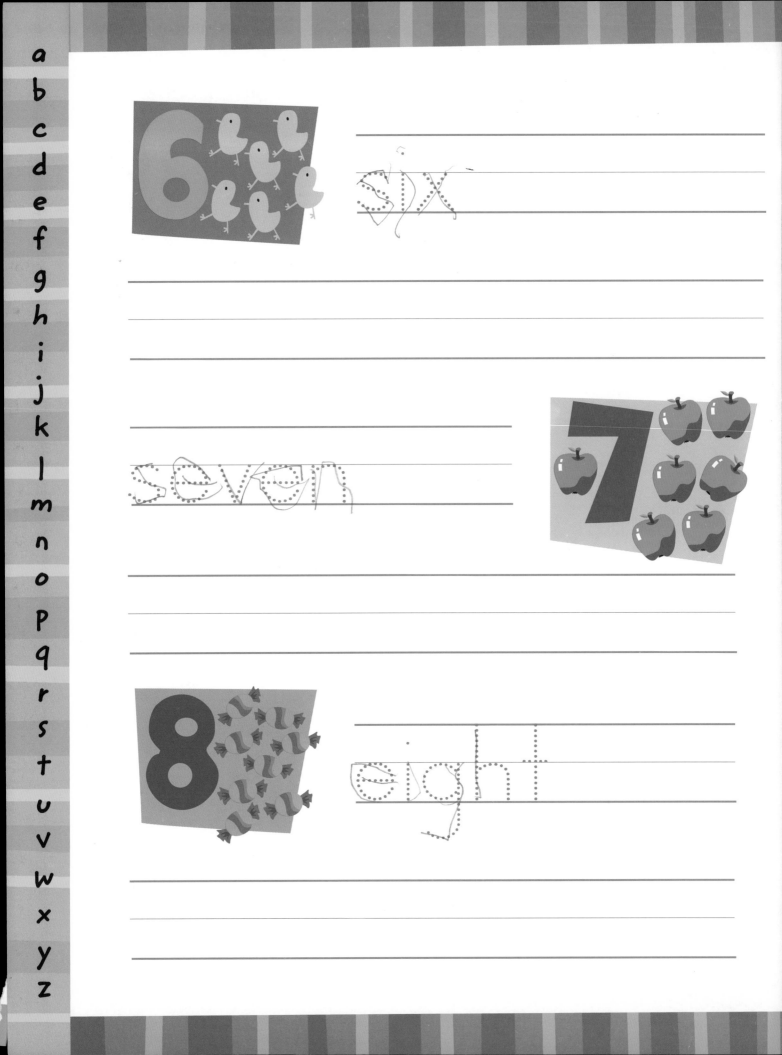

nine

9

10

ten

eleven

11

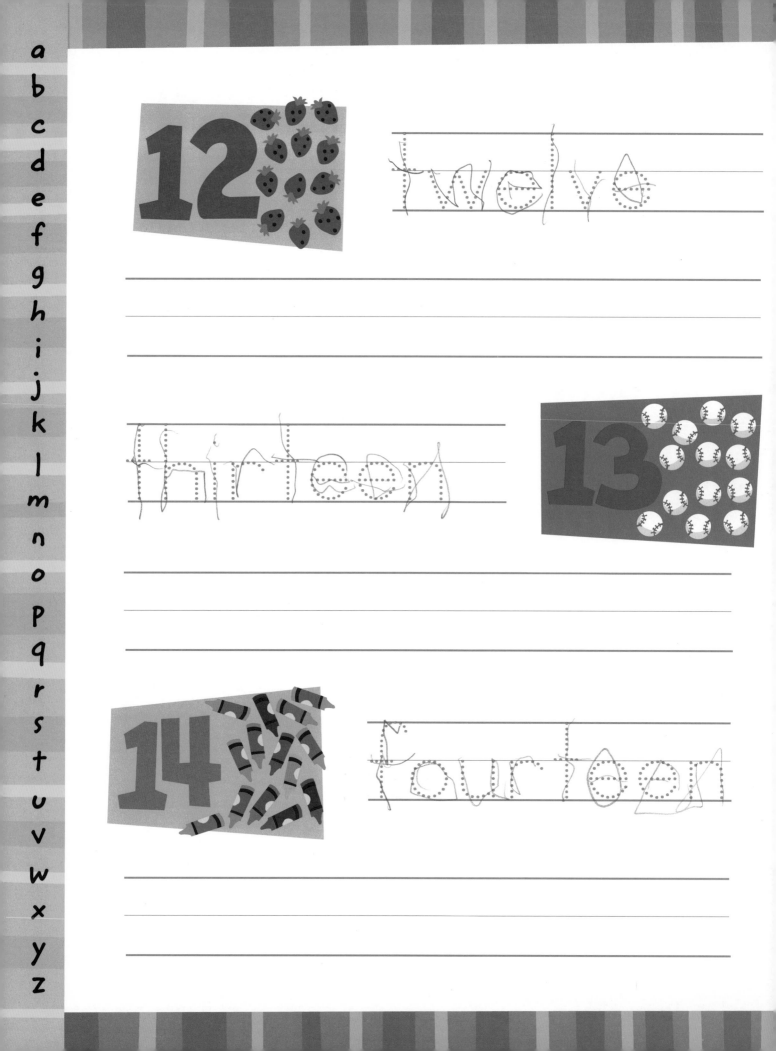

a
b
c
d
e
f
g
h
i
j
k
l
m
n
o
p
q
r
s
t
u
v
w
x
y
z

12   twelve

thirteen   13

14   fourteen

fifteen

15

16

sixteen

seventeen

17

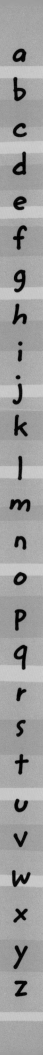

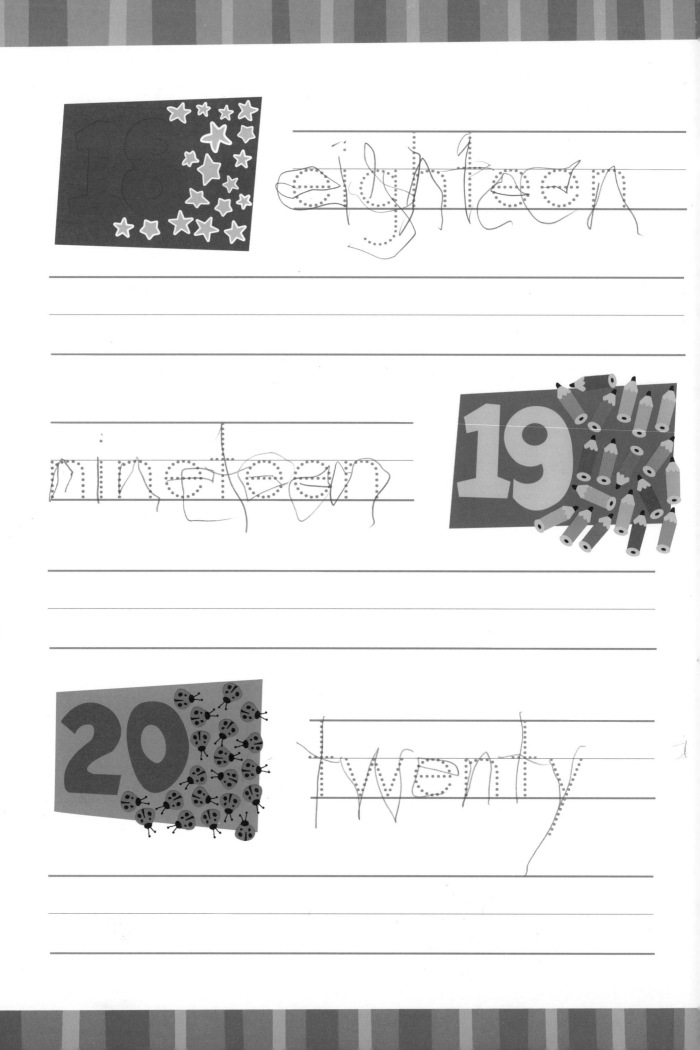

eighteen

nineteen

twenty

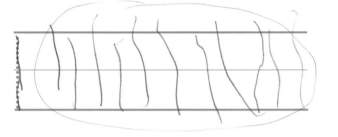
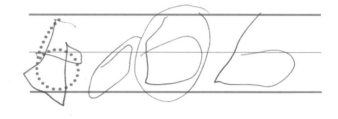
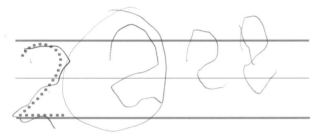
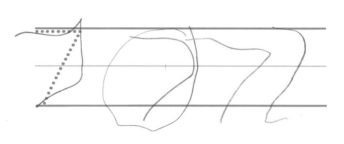

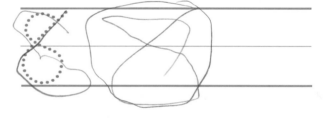
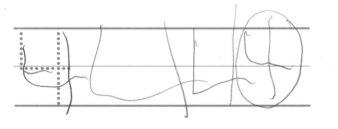
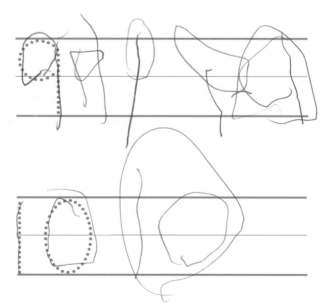
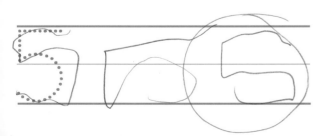

Your Body

Trace and write.

leg   leg

arm   arm

ear   ear

eye   eye yyy

a b c d e f g h i j k l m n o p q r s t u v w x y z

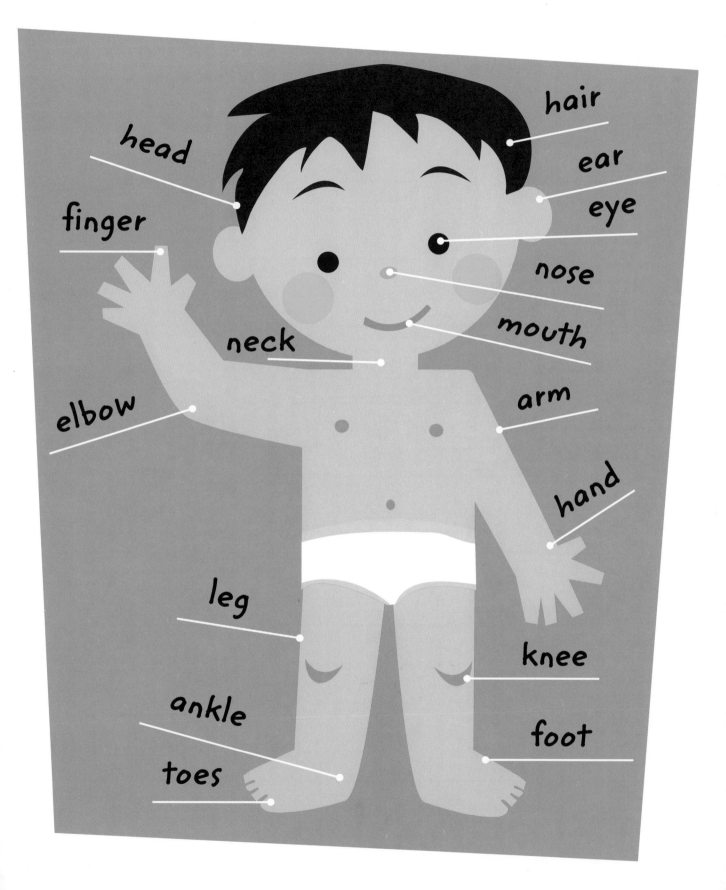

a b c d e f g h i j k l m n o p q r s t u v w x y z

hand

finger

foot

toes

nose

hair

knee

neck

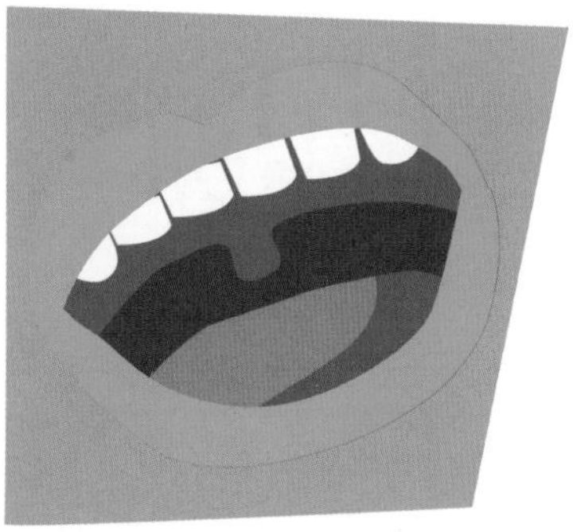

mouth

head

Food

Trace and write.

fruit

milk

egg

juice

fish

bread

rice

meat

dessert

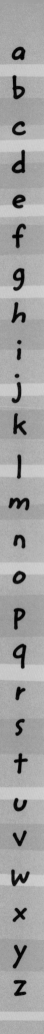

Days of the Week

Trace and write.

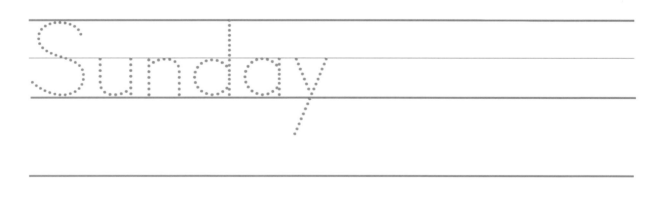

Sunday

Monday

Monday

Tuesday

Tuesday

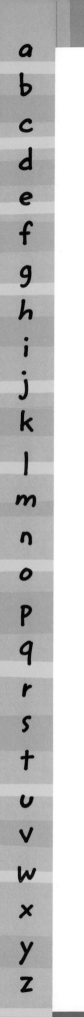

Wednesday

Wednesday

Thursday

Thursday

Friday

Friday

Saturday

Saturday

Months of the Year

Trace and write.

January

January

February

February

March

March

April

May

June

a b c d e f g h i j k l m n o p q r s t u v w x y z

July

July

August

August

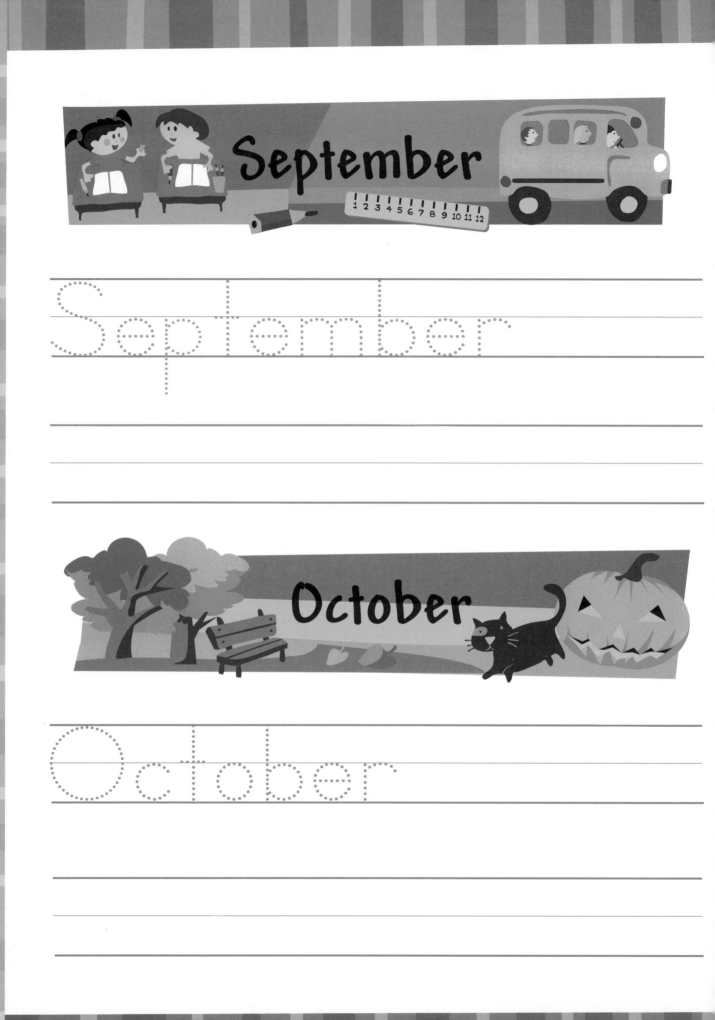

a b c d e f g h i j k l m n o p q r s t u v w x y z

September

September

October

October

November

November

December

December

a b c d e f g h i j k l m n o p q r s t u v w x y z

Weather

Trace and write.

sunny

snowy

cloudy

rainy

windy

a
b
c
d
e
f
g
h
i
j
k
l
m
n
o
p
q
r
s
t
u
v
w
x
y
z

Shapes

Trace and write.

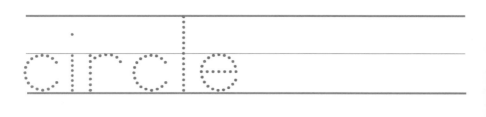

circle

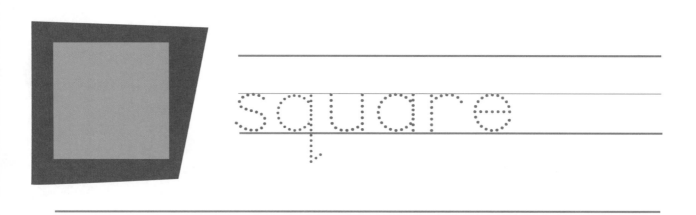

square

triangle

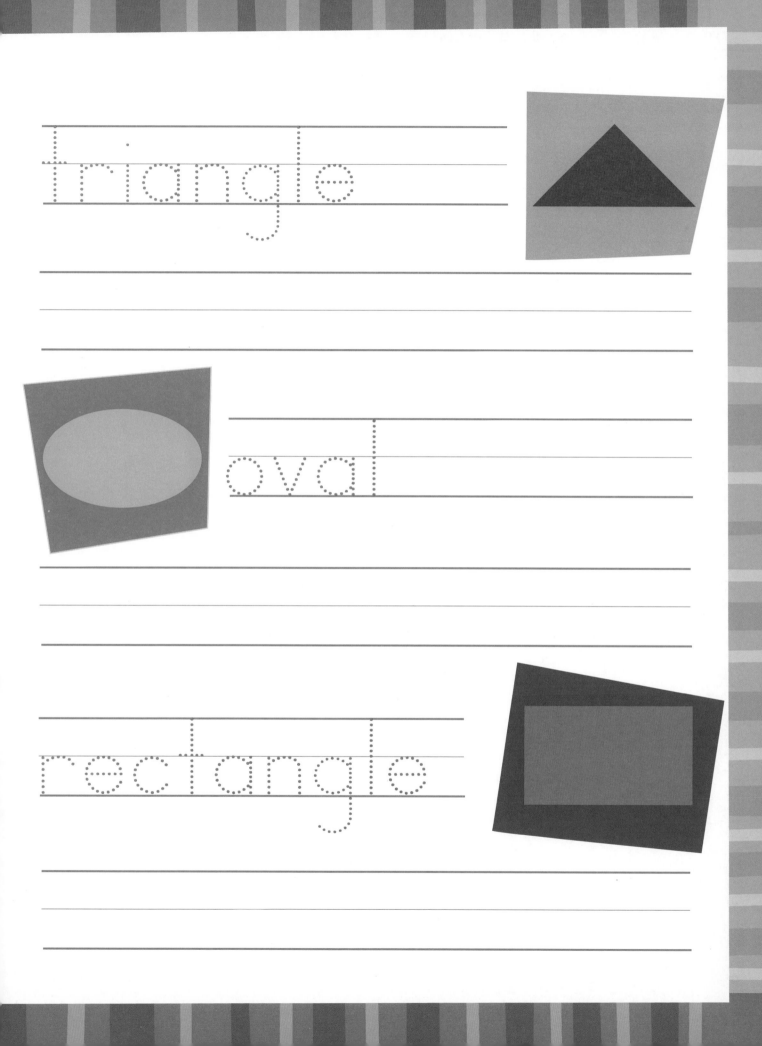

oval

rectangle

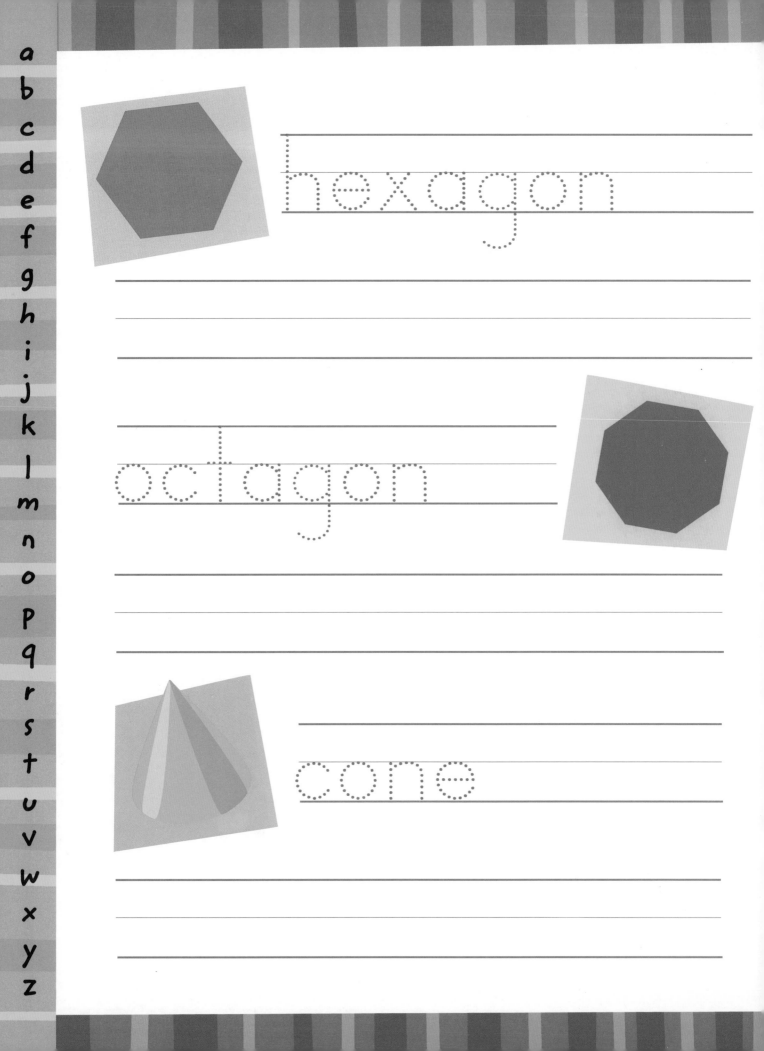

a b c d e f g h i j k l m n o p q r s t u v w x y z

hexagon

octagon

cone

cylinder

cube

pyramid

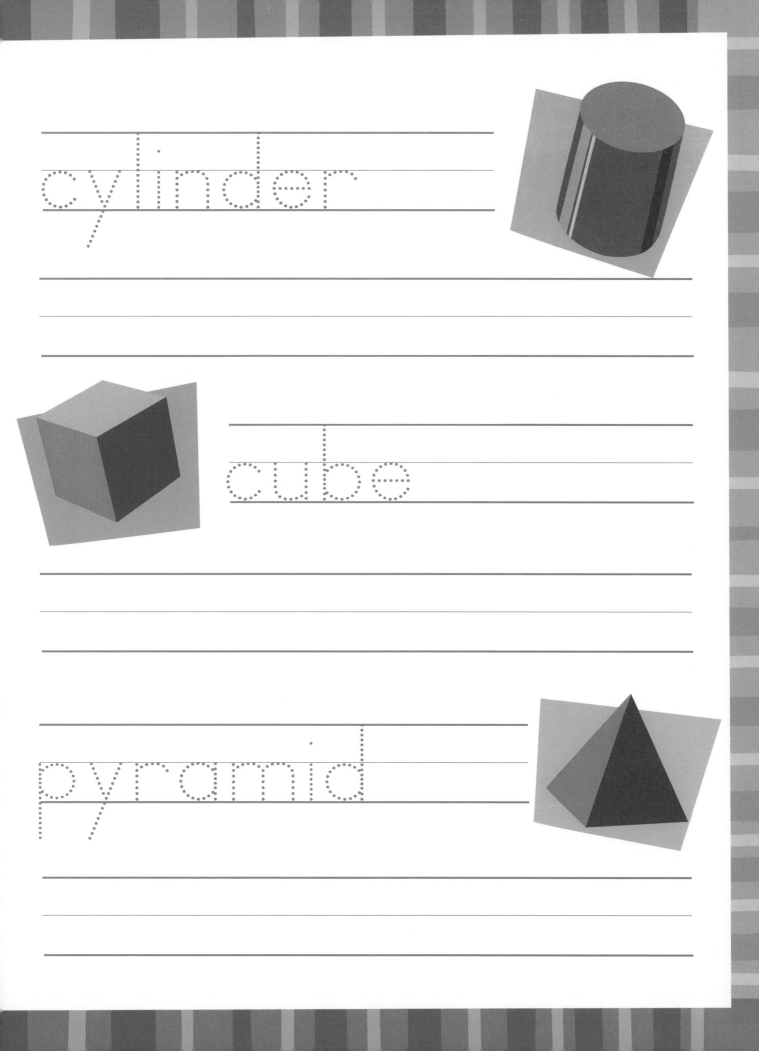

People

Trace and write.

mother

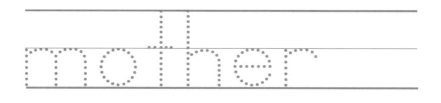

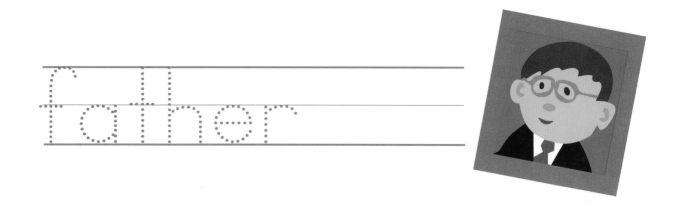

father

a b c d e f g h i j k l m n o p q r s t u v w x y z

sister

brother

cousin

grandmother

grandfather

aunt

uncle

police officer

firefighter

teacher

a b c d e f g h i j k l m n o p q r s t u v w x y z

Signs

Trace and write.

stop

yield

go

exit

bus stop

hospital

girls

boys

At the Office

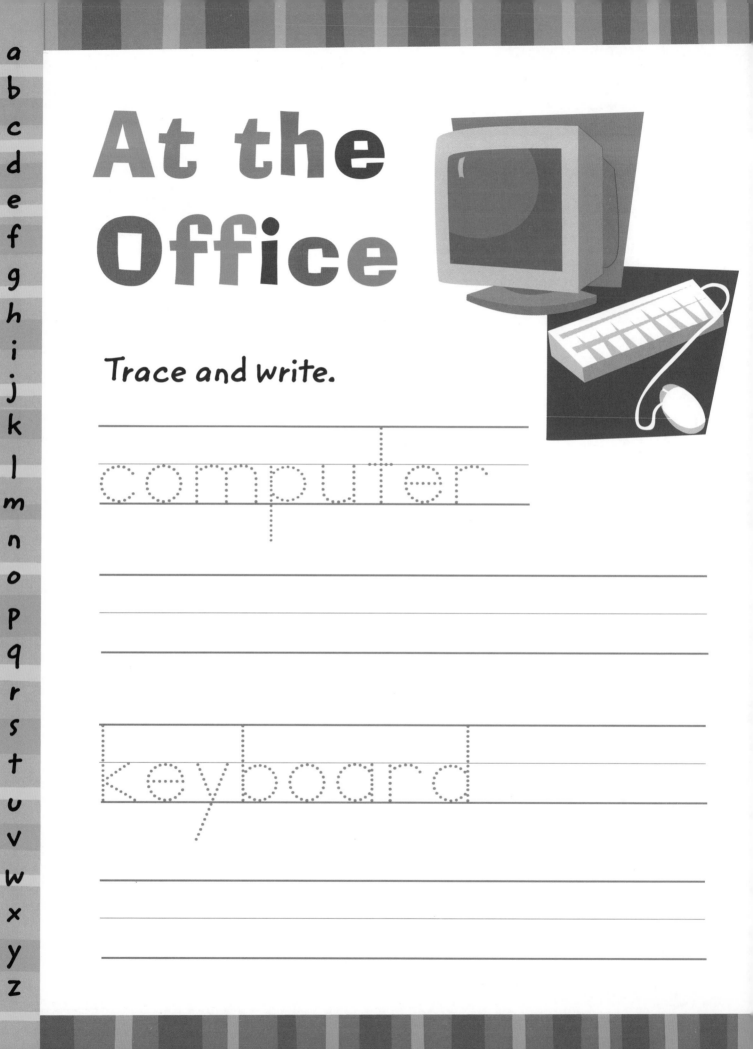

Trace and write.

computer

keyboard

printer

disc

calculator

At Home

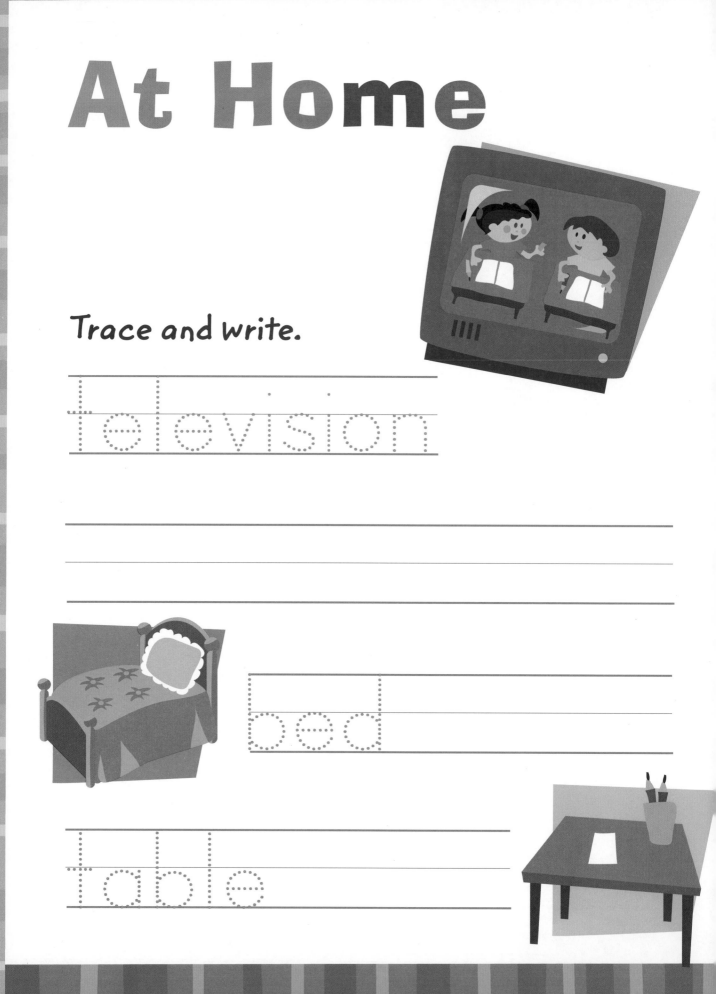

Trace and write.

television

bed

table

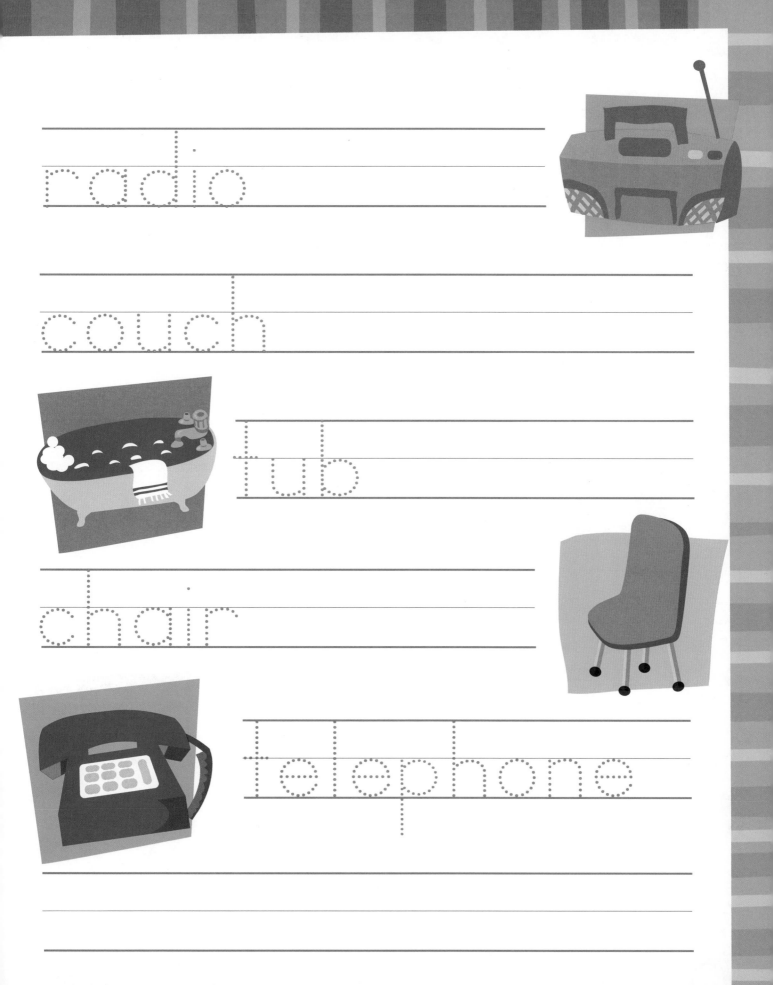

radio

couch

tub

chair

telephone

Things That Go

Trace and write.

truck

train

car

bus

jeep

a
b
c
d
e
f
g
h
i
j
k
l
m
n
o
p
q
r
s
t
u
v
w
x
y
z

bicycle

boat

airplane

fire truck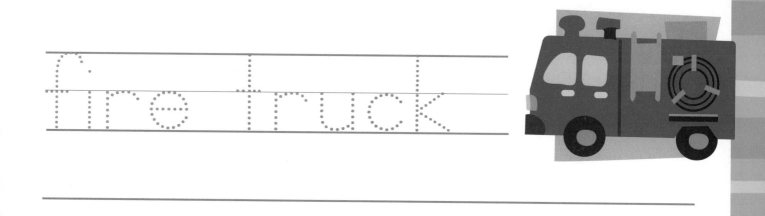

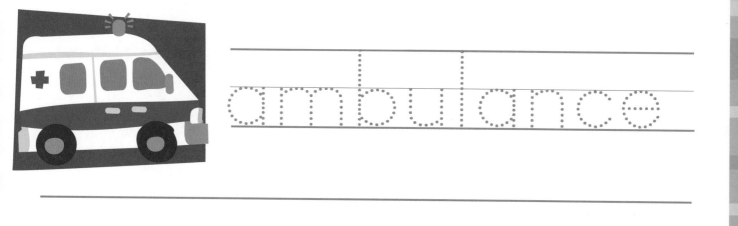 ambulance

motorcycle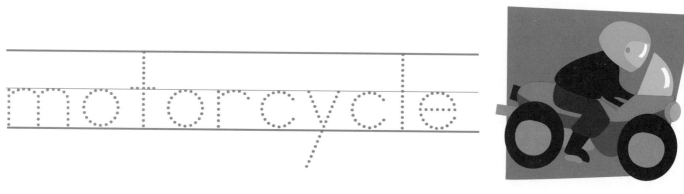

Where?

Trace and write.

over

under

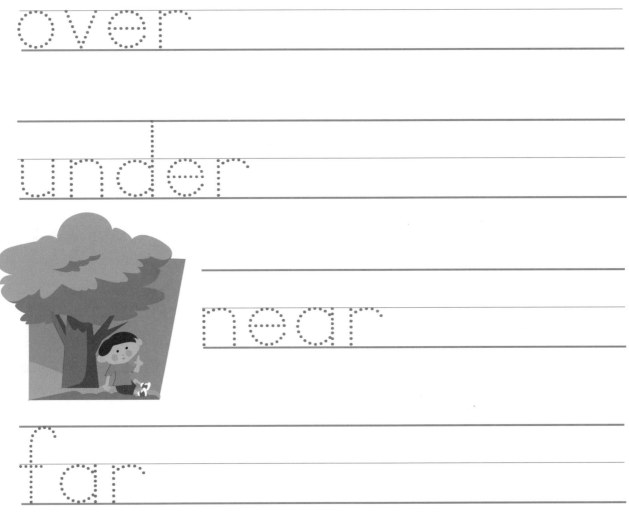

near

far

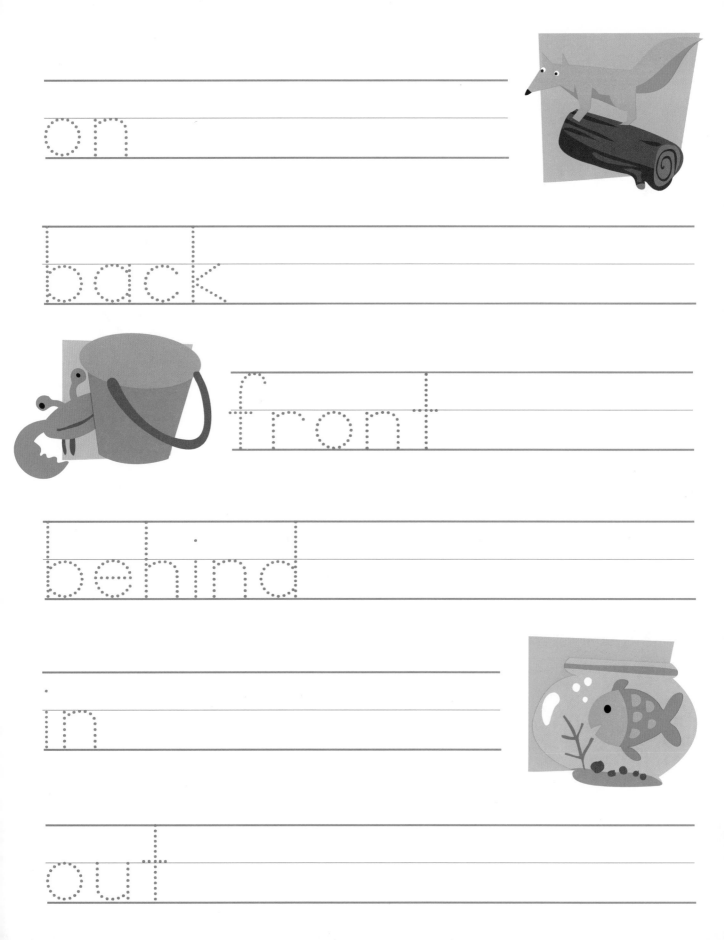

on

back

front

behind

in

out

Our World

Trace and write.

earth

river

lake

ocean

mountain

sky

stars

sun

cloud

a
b
c
d
e
f
g
h
i
j
k
l
m
n
o
p
q
r
s
t
u
v
w
x
y
z

More Sight Words

Trace and write
the word.

That is a flag.

That

This is a dog.

This

I **have** candy!

have

I can write this **word**.

_ _ _ _ _ _ _ _ _ _ _ _ _ _ _ _ _ _

word

What does a pig say?

What

We are **all** at the playground.

all

We **were** learning in school.

_ _ _ _ _ _ _ _ _ _ _ _ _ _ _ _ _ _

were

I **can** ride a bike.

_ _ _ _ _ _ _ _ _ _ _ _ _ _ _ _ _ _

can

We are going to **their** house.

their

We flew in a plane to get **there**.

there

I **will** share my toys.

will

I **see** a cat.

see

My grandmother **said** hello.

said

Which **way** is the fire station?

way

Could I have more rice, please?

Could

Which season do you like best?

Which

I got a letter **from** my friend.

from

May I **call** my mother?

call

a b c d e f g h i j k l m n o p q r s t u v w x y z

Who is at the door?

May I have a cup of **water**?

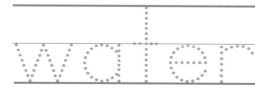

What is on television **now**?

Let's find my doll **and** play.

The snake is long.

Did the girl jump?

_____

Di̇d

I will **get** my fish some food.

_____

get

We **come** to the city.

_____

come

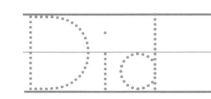

I **made** a drawing.

_____

made

I want to learn **more** words!

_____

more

GREAT JOB!

_____

_____

_____

date

_____

_____

_____

first name

_____

_____

last name

★ ★ ★ ★ ★ **I Can READ** ★ ★ ★ ★ ★
Over 200 Sight Words